Walking Sideways

Robert Carey

BookLeaf Publishing

India | USA | UK

Walking Sideways © 2025 Robert Carey

All rights reserved.

No part of this publication may be reproduced, stored in a retrieval system, or transmitted, in any form or by any means, electronic, mechanical, photocopying, recording or otherwise, without the prior written permission of the presenters.

Robert Carey asserts the moral right to be identified as the author of this work.

Presentation by *BookLeaf Publishing*

Web: www.bookleafpub.com

E-mail: info@bookleafpub.com

ISBN: 9789358316223

First edition 2025

To everyone who has suffered cancer's cruel torment, and to everyone who will sadly end up facing it. Never give up.

Accept the negative.

Embrace it.

Use it.

The sun will shine on us again.

ACKNOWLEDGEMENTS

This wouldn't have been possible without BookLeaf and their wonderful poetry challenge. Endless thanks also go out to my friends who supported me through everything, especially the ones who were forced to read my drafts. Deep gratitude to everyone who walked with me, whatever direction we were headed in, whether it was for a minute or a millennia. Thanks and appreciation to all the medical workers and mental health workers who help people like me every day.

Love and thanks to Talia, my sunflower, for supporting me and helping my withered passion for writing bloom anew.

Lastly, my most heartfelt thanks to my mother, Kathy, who is the strongest person I know. Without her unshakeable support, I would have fallen at countless hurdles.

PREFACE

After moving to the Netherlands in 2018, Robert Carey went on a new journey of ups and downs. There were many happy days lived in those times, but he did not expect depression to rear its ugly head or that after battling through it, a cancer diagnosis would knock the wind back out of him again.

Having weathered an operation, recovery and chemotherapy, he was lucky enough to get COVID twice. Following the end of a relationship and coming to terms with life as a survivor, he chose to move back to the UK in 2023 and subsequently lapsed back into depression. This book is born of his pain but also his resilience. It is his own version of therapy and his non-sugar-coated open-armed hug to all those who have been before him and all those yet to come.

This book features smatterings of nautical themes, animals, and mythology – such as crabs and the mythical Hydra – to represent cancer and depression respectively.

End

I wake at dawn. Rust-orange light comes in a smear
Round the edges of my plain white blinds and under the door.
My partner still slumbers, pressed in our cat's cashmere
Fur. 'They look warm', I think, as I swing my feet to the floor.

Today is significant. It is a day for change.
I know what to expect; it's all been made crystal clear.
I hum some basic tune, as I open the drawer
Where my socks swim in an unpaired mess; there's no order here.

We ride to the castle. The sun stretches the clouds to peer
Down on our approach as dying summer winds roar.
I shudder. It's cold, yet his hot gaze pierces like a spear
Through my gut. His victory, but I don't keep score.

The waiting room is neatly painted with a thin veneer
Of relaxation. I sit, feeling saddle sore.
My eyes wander to the various plants, grown far from here
In some green place. Yet now they sit and move no more.

My left sock has a butterfly motif, but for
The right sock, I chose ravens. I wear odd socks without fear.
I smile intermittently. Facial tug-of-war
Whilst we wait, until my appointment breaks this atmosphere.

It's receiving day. Why they picked me is unclear
But I'm not alone. Each day they choose winners galore.
I'm to receive a gift. Now, you might think, 'oh dear
It must be some prank'! No, it's real. It isn't some folklore.

Some people receive hummingbirds to drink their tears
Like nectar. Some get sweet-smelling flowers or precious ores.
So as they unveil my prize, I prepare to cheer
But they stop. Glances exchanged. I break

Eye contact in this uncomfortable silence

  A glance to the side and what seems like violence

 Must have occurred because there is dark blood

  Adorning the floor; from out the door, it's trailing like mud

  But almost coagulated, somewhat blackened and viscous like tar

  Or perhaps treacle. It leads to my foot where something bizarre

  Though maybe unexpected is a better term for what I see

  When looking down. The doctor is still talking to me.

But her words seem to hang still in the air

  Just long enough that I might reach to pluck them like hair

But they slip through my fingers as sand through a glass

  How they glisten in the half-light, like finely polished brass.

Suddenly,
 They shatter.
  On the sterile floor.
   Pieces form a pattern like the blood from before.

At last, my senses return with a quiet stab.
Gripping inseparable, yet painless, to my ankle is a small crab.

*****

O, Gentle Spirit, you sweep me away,
Across canals in the blink of an eye.
O'er the ocean to where my home does lay,
The heady scent of nostalgia floating by.

Atop a high cliff, early autumn mists
Press themselves against silent, dull grey waves
That lap at the rocks as though they were kissed
By kindly sea wisps from ancient sea caves.

Believe not this mockery of the mind.
Peel back these frigid waters to see death,
Endless bodies churned, a salt net to bind.
Upon the cliff, I wait with ragged breath.

The crab sits with me. I leap and descend.
We watch together as I meet my End.

After The Fall

Cycling past fields on a static bike,
Where tulips of blue and orange grow
With dew-kissed petals that sway feather-like.
A storm raged last night, but I did not know.

This regimented horticulture is grand,
There is no doubt that beneath this flat soil
A golden bulb of strength lies – though access is banned.
It's the same old field, yet somehow harder to toil.

These chewed lips taste of cinnamon, but the flavour fades,
Not much, though it slows the rotation of my countless
Windmill sails, bearing the elements over the decades.
The tulips scuttle to view me, how I cycle aimless.

I imagine myself as one of them. Standing tall and proud.
Perhaps I'd best go on, though I don't know how far this bike lane
Will take me. Above drifts a darkening cloud.
I sigh. Looks like rain.

September Stroll

Amber leaves flutter
Caught by a gentle wind's bite
Summer meets its end

Down by the canal
The rabbit's taupe fur grows thick
Summer meets its end

Through the mottled trees
Sunlight fades to mellow haze
Summer meets its end

Upon the crisp heath
Old shrubs burst into deep purple
Autumn's born again

The Forge

Upon our anvils, we lay
　As the hammer blows,
Whether it strikes true or nay
　Our Father Time knows;
Such are His famed powers
　Of pasts and futures,
That both droughts and showers
　He threads through us like sutures.
And no mortal ever shall tell whether tears flow
　from His sapphire eyes.

Within this forge the harsh sounds
　Dull our active minds,
Repeating with rhythmic pounds
　The soul it soon grinds;
But for those who relish fear
　With eyes cast up above,
In that endless void may peer
　Upon His Precious craft of Love;
And all the while His shapeless shadows flow
　towards their now unguarded prize.

Recklessly Elusive Mind

Eyes close but dreams evade.
Dreams won't come; you must first wake.
First Day is here; they hand you a spade.
A whole lot of digging, but you'll get a break.

Slow your heart, but don't keep score.
Keep your eyes sharp; there's no second glance.
Second Day is here; you stand on the shore.
The defences you made won't stand a chance.

From the ocean, this serpent of fear attacks.
Fear the Hydra's poison breath, burning third-degree.
Third Day is here; see how time contracts.
Time to battle this behemoth of the undersea.

Vengeful Hera of Olympus now laughs at your expense.
Your attention drifts; her tactics are fourth-rate.
Fourth Day descends with the weight of prison bars.
Prison of the mind is where this Goddess tries to stab.
To focus on the Hydra is to forget about her crab.
Her scuttling servant that you must fling into the stars.
The crab bites your feet, so small yet such weight.
Such battles require Herculean strength too immense.

The Fisherman

'The crab has to go'; of that, there was no doubt.
So I floated between hospital rooms, where various kinds
Of seafaring folk ran tests, casting their nets wide.
It seemed so clinical and serious – you'd think someone had died!
Some days I'd tread water amongst the seaweed vines
But often, I didn't dare let my imagination swim out.

We sailed far too often to these weather-tested minds.
Thick fog filled my head until I could hardly hear them shout
Their expert advice; my brain a slice of battered fish fried.
I gave so much blood, each needle cast aught find my waters dried!
Presumably, this precious fluid found use as chum throughout
My intestinal depths, dredging to see what science finds.

The ship's cook explained the type of diet I should eat.
'No shellfish'? I joke. Everyone laughs at my jokes, at least
On the surface. These types remain professional above the waves.
My maritime crustacean specialist knows how our enemy behaves.
Her title is a bit of a mouthful but her words are warmly fleeced
Like a heavy jumper, into which my cold weariness can retreat.

The Fisherman arrives and regards me as a puzzle to be pieced.
His eyes slice me up and down, as though a scalpel across meat
From his catch. Despite this, I feel calm; it's not my flesh he craves.
When our long journey begins, it shall be my life that he saves.
He scrubs his hands and disinfects his hooks. There'll be no defeat
Once he takes the helm, I'm optimistic that we won't need the priest.

Diving For Tumours

The sun has not risen, yet the harbour swims with life.
Routine safety checks for a voyage meticulously planned.
The dreaded date is upon us; I'll soon go under the nautical knife
For the second time, the first was so very long ago;
That memory now sits, nestled in the rock pools of my past.

The ocean stretches out to shake hands with the sky.
On a day like today, such pleasantries seem grand.
But as the light of dawn creeps near, the sun will pry
This union apart, the ink-black void recedes slow,
Until our outlook is clear. Anchor up; it's time to go at last.

We head through to the ship's waiting room.
All three of us sit, but in honesty, I'd rather stand.
Surgical staff smile politely, though thoughts conjure a tomb
Deep below these dark waters, over which we flow,
And I know I should feel safe, but my heart beats so fast.

Tides begin to shift
As words take on a different tone.
The crew beckon us on deck
Where the swirling winds have grown.
I knew the procedures and rules
But still, my heart sinks like a stone.
My mother and girlfriend
Must transfer back to shore, leaving me alone.

I change my clothes,
Putting on my hospital diving gown,
With precision as shown.

The weather is like my woes,
A grey onslaught that threatens to drown,
With a bitter cold, cutting to bone.

The open water echoes,
As thunder claps and lightning arcs down,
With heavy clouds that groan.

And now heaven bestows
A mighty deluge of ice all around,
With hailstones as though thrown.
Each strike on the sea a rift,
An elemental flock to claw and peck,
As the surgical team prepares their tools.
The water's surface boils, and I prepare to descend.

Into this bleak scene now strides
The Fisherman, with confidence unmatched.
My storm-wracked mind feels damp and patched,
Until they lay me down and my wrist is scratched
By some sort of hook, and my tension subsides.

A diving mask is placed over my face
And tightened, there's no urge to resist.
The boat is slowly enveloped by mist,
Until my salt-sprayed soul feels kissed
By some ethereal warmth, settling softly in place.

Monochrome gloom still grips the sky
In place, whilst winds surge and protest.
But the cold cannot find purchase within my breast,
No matter how many times it may try to infest
The serene silence, here in the storm's eye.

I barely notice as they lift and push me
Overboard, plummeting headfirst toward the swell.
Instead of crashing into a murky cyclone hell,
I slip gently underneath and sink slow as if gel
Had replaced these depths, as far as the eye can see.

Deeper and deeper I let myself glide
Towards light, now tentatively shining below.
The grey and black retreat as colours overflow,
Bursting bright and darting to and fro
Swim such divine fish with purpose and pride.

Entranced by crimsons and sapphires and gold
I float, blissfully unaware of what lies in wait.
Half dreaming, I realise that I am the bait,
Its colossal shadow appears and there's no mistake
That this giant awakens – what a horror to behold.

This clawed behemoth is my unwanted crab
That clings vice-like, with a wretched smell.
In the blink of an eye, chunks shatter from its shell,
As The Fisherman's harpoons skewer and expel
This mutated monster, as though ripping a scab.

Its death throes sting me to the core
Like poison, a final gift to secrete.
The surgeon cleaves the beast from my intestinal meat.
The bowel resection surgery is finally complete
And the tumour scuttles no more.

The Tide Pool

Faint tapping from trapped fingers.
Tubes find their fixed trenches.
Time freezes, then fire trickles,
Flowing from friend to foe.

Fledglings taking flight to find
Tattered feathers that tumble down,
Then fracture, to diminish.
Finally, triumph. Grateful smiles.

Broken chains fall forcefully.
Faces gleaming, hope gathering,
But the tapping continues.
Feelings turn. Pyrrhic victory.

Querying eyes want a confirmation,
Passing over the inseparable fallen.
Surface tension returns, yet beneath
Hope sinks unseen. Clinging to fear.

The Crab Who Came To Tea

Once there was a young man called Rob, who sat
Having tea in the kitchen with his girlfriend and cat.
He was thinking, 'rhyming couplets are a thing to deplore',
When all of a sudden came a knock on their front door.

'I wonder who that can be'? he said, with some debate,
'It can't be the milkman because it's not 1968'.
They had not invited anyone and their neighbours had a key,
Still, it's rude to make callers wait, so they all went to see.

Rob opened the door to find a small, oval-bodied crab.
A silence quickly descended that itched like a scab.
'Uh... of course, come in...' said Rob awkwardly,
As the crustacean entered and clacked its claws with glee.

So there they sat, with palpable tension like a powder keg,
Until Rob motioned to the food, 'Would you like a boiled egg'?
The creature took them all, peeling them one by one,
Scattering eggshells across the floor once its task was done.

'Maybe it's allergic'! they joked to hide their surprise.
The crab didn't eat the eggs despite the hunger in its eyes.
'Perhaps you'd like some pancakes instead'? they enquired,
But the crab didn't touch them, and Rob's demeanour expired.

'Look here, you little shrimp; you're meant to eat all of this!
Then I'd offer you a drink, and you'd accept it with bliss'!
The crab refused all their spreads, meats and cheese,
Even sausages and potatoes mashed with kale didn't please.

Instead, the crab then slowly destroyed
All the things that they liked and enjoyed.
He consumed their energy throughout the day,
Then at night, he ate their dreams away.

'Isn't it supposed to be a tiger'? their cat asked in dismay.
'I didn't know you could talk...' Rob would say.
'This is probably a dream then; it's all in your head'.
But Rob was still sad and spent more time in bed.

At night, in the small hours, he would try to ignore
All the negativity that the crab would pour
Into his thoughts where, like a spore,
It could grow and mutate as before.

It seemed that Rob's patience eventually could not
Do without distractions which untied the knot,
That weaved itself into some hidden spot
Until he overlooked a small part and forgot,
That whilst he treads water, his insides could rot
So he tried to plough on and not bemoan his lot,
And he put on the best brave face he had got,
Or his mind may slow and thicken and clot.

The tumour was gone but the doctors had said
That little crabs might have sneaked off and fled,
So instead of fishing for every small thread
It was time to throw dynamite into the sea instead.
And a demolitions expert described the voyage ahead
But to be honest, it all went straight over Rob's head,
And, as this is a children's book parody, best not to spread,
Intense chemotherapy details. We'll leave that unsaid.

So in the end the crab never really came to tea,
Though its memory did damage Rob couldn't foresee.
During that winter with infusions and pills,
The frost attacked most of the daffodils.

In the months to come, things would struggle to bloom.
With only dead seeds left to exhume.

December Downpour

Burnt grey skies above,
Dark flames of ice rekindle.
Not yet halfway done.

Warm chocolate milk.
Kind faces seek assurance,
Given heartily.

Routine flows deeply
As Fear still stalks the hallways,
Glancing at his watch.

Back in the canteen
A Christmas tree burns with hope,
Whilst I drown in coal.

Fibbing

Hmm.
Cold
Outside.
Winter has
Begun his long siege.
Time to make – ah sh*t, caught COVID.

Hmm.
No
Matter,
I can mix
Face masks and mince pies.
Nothing can crush my Christmas joy.

Hmm.
It
Appears
My taste buds
Have broken. Now all
Food is cardboard and tear-flavoured.

Hmm.
Now
That I
Think about it,
Tears are quite salty.
If only I could still taste salt.

Hmm.
I
Digress.
I should be
Writing poetry
With a deep yet subtle meaning.

Hmm.
Ah!
Tiger,
Burning bright,
In the – ah shit, this
Is just Blake's 'The Tyger' poem.

Hmm.
Can
We still
Print this part?
He's been dead for a
While now, I think we'll be okay.

Hmm.
I'll
Write a
Better poem!
He rhymes the words 'eye'
And 'symmetry', such mockery!

Hmm.
Time
To get
Serious.
How hard can it be?
That's rhetorical; don't answer.

O'
Heart,
Spin a
Silken web
Within my dark chest.
Threads twitch; nostalgia leaves its nest.

O'
What
A feast!
We await
Such memories sweet.
Threads tangle; time has come to eat.

O'
Gods,
Such vile
Bitter blood
From this truth now seeps.
Threads burn, silently the heart weeps.

Hmm.
That
Was great!
Didn't even need
To get naked or see angels.

Hmm.
I
Do not
Mean to brag,
But this poetry
Stuff is so incredibly easy – ah shit...

Mother

Karma. It's a concept that avoids my understanding.
A saint I am not, we all indulge in vice,
Though my mental and medical maladies seem unfair.
Here I sit and rot, poison itching through veins like ice.
Yearning to converse when words shift and slur.

Yet through the iron clouds overhead she breaks.
Hastened to my side, made of hardy Northern stock,
This woman smiles and sends shadows to the abyss.
All the pills I'll abide, to feel the warmth that laugh can unlock.
Karma. I'll try every day to deserve her.

Elapse

Take down the cracked clock
Still ticking with guarded groans.
How its seconds send
A sharp chill through brittle bones.
How its minutes mock
The life of diligent drones.
How its brackets bend
From the weight its case condones.
Unable to tock.

In Tandem

Love is the bicycle wheel bearing your weight.
You blow air from chapped lips, just enough to inflate
So that the tyre grips and the moon can rotate,
Through phases to an eclipse where things can deviate.

The pressure may drop and make you quite irate.
Pedalling insults and quips, back and forth they oscillate
Until flat your tyre slips, eyes wide as pupils dilate,
Through tender fingertips a lasting pain can resonate.

All may seem lost, and perhaps it's now too late.
But two wheels form partnerships, so your chained fate
May yet weather such blips, if we can learn to tolerate,
The jagged spoke that rips like chalk across slate.

A pristine bicycle is a miracle that we venerate.
Glossy paint on a frame so slender as a dancer's hips,
The urge to start riding is one that is easy to sate,
But a closer look reveals rust from which off-brown water drips.

Routine maintenance cannot continue to wait.
You're likely no mechanic but your duty doesn't skip,
Blemishes have their charm and needn't lead to hate,
A little bit of care may weather every peak and dip.

Love is the bicycle wheel bearing your weight.
Yet passion is the journey it helps you create,
Commitment is not slowing when the rains won't abate,
Empathy is knowing that the route is not always straight,
Happiness comes when the view is one you can appreciate.

March Comes In Like A Lion

When March awakens,
Breath cold and indifferent,
Ice still claims my veins.

I don't count the days.
Dreams, as the thick sky above,
Prone to remain grey.

Colours burst swiftly,
Roaring for change. Determined.
Staunchly unaware.

Silent, they wither.
Most pleasant memories do.
No lamb to be seen.

Gratitude

Grated cheese that cascades straight from the packet.
Reliable nurses who care for me day after day.
Ambling through the forest wearing three layers and a jacket.
Tireless medical minds whom no doubt we underpay.

Internet connections that mean I'm never truly alone.
Tubes that pour preventative poison relatively quickly.
Umpteen cards and gifts as people make their love known.
Detestable amounts of pills that make me feel sickly.

Even though my face may often look sour,
Not a day goes by without an inward smile.
Despite the shadows that creep and devour,
Laughter emerges from each daily trial.

Eternal thanks to every single soul,
Stalwart champions standing unafraid.
Seasons may take their toll, but your warmth will be repaid.

Bittersweet Departure

Unfortunately, peanut butter.
I swap shades of red, white and blue.
Another roll of the dice.
Four wheels instead of two.
Re-stiffen my lip.
I pack my weight.
But I'll leave
My heart
Here.

Sleeping Tiger

Silently twitching the tiger dreams,
Lazily drifting down slumberous streams,
Even I could not accurately foretell,
Ever when this saffron beast will wake.
Patiently the sun waits with dull ember ache.
Irrecusable stripes like prison bars compel,
Now observe as the feline chest does rise and swell,
Great paws sprawling and shallow breaths it does take.

Time floats without effort on this lucid trail,
Imbued by the moonlight and guided by the tail.
Giants of red and rubber would glance,
Elastic whiskers invite monkeys to dance,
Razor teeth to marshmallow if given the chance.

Forces

Pushing…
Against the flow.

Blissfully unaware
Of the ravenous undertow.
Rising.

June Jigsaw

Dusting off the box.
A familiar puzzle,
No timer to set.

Hands moving slowly,
Too hot to fish for pieces.
Commitment fading.

The picture's the same,
But now the edges won't fit.
How the net tightens.

Misprinted segments.
Soon the tide will wash back in,
And I pray for floods.

The Slake

A dull ache.
Rhythmic, yet shifting,
Ornate-stained orange bunting, drifting,
On a breeze, picking up pace before the slake.

Nowhere to fly, as dizzying spirits rise,
Languishing beneath amber waves, fired with inaudible cries,
The napkin descends. The ache is gone.

Pie

Oh, Pie.
Your consumption is my destiny,
Your presentation is heavenly,
Your aroma, a melody,
Your perfection, a rarity,
Your presence brings clarity,
Your absence brings misery,
Your recipe, kept under lock and key,
Your pastry, a beacon of rigidity,
Your importance, renowned historically,
Your flavours hit like artillery,
Your filling, sweet or savoury,
The latter with gravy? Obligatory,
The former with cream? Ecstasy,
You're basically a substitute for therapy,
And if need be, even gluten or dairy-free,
We can't underestimate your gravity,
When it comes to the power of your industry,
Production, packing, storage, delivery,
All taken for granted when somewhat hungrily,
We place you in the oven and delighted we see,
Your edges turn a shade of deep golden honey,
Your praises I could sing out eternally,
You might even be immune to entropy,
Such is your undisputed energy,
Though now I think about it, chemically,
I probably shouldn't leave you openly,
Where bacteria or, worse, an enemy,
Could heinously, with much jealousy,
Take you far away from me!

Where was I... ah yes.

Oh, Pie, I declare gratefully,
How I long to sample thee,
The time has come to–
Alas. You have gone cold.

Damn you, Pie.

Nostalgia

Petals suspended
In the ice of years gone by
As sweet scents secrete
And soft colours soothe the eye
But you reach with hands aflame

The Anchor

You think his gaze cast low,
He that is shackled by the Anchor?
Pulling at the head as cumbrous cargo.
Stock to be taken, or taken from stock.

Your pity prevents no harm,
Nor cleanses the shank of vile rancour.
Flakes of skin liberated from his raw palms.
Hate fills your throat; muscles start to lock.

One arm now rises as the other arm falls,
He laughs heartily as his pupils dilate.
You wince at this heavy burden of weight.
Yet it is his crown, and the storm calls.

Work To Be Done

The harvest approaches.
I'm the seeds that I planted.
    The fence encroaches.
I'm the panel that is slanted.

    When the breeze shifts,
I'm the crops that are yearning.
    When the rain drifts,
I'm the fields that are burning.

    The grim darkness draws ever near
As the weary hands still toil.
    The ragged sun starts to smear
As the stars expand and boil.

    Now the clouds crumble like old brick,
As distant trees bow to the floor.
    Now the crane's wings melt and stick,
As farmhands rush to judge and score.
    But I rake my hand through soil ever thick,
    And dutifully I begin to plant seeds once more.

September Swim

The water is cold.
Why did I let summer end
Before plunging in?

Gulls flap silent wings.
No roar of salt spray to be
Heard from muted waves.

The bodies still churn.
Unseen until this mirrored
Surface is broken.

Thoughts drift unanswered.
Yet I walk on the fallen
And ask – am I next?

Burnt Past

Pry the door from its frame.
This shadow provides no shade,
A debt unpaid,
Splintered hands conveyed,
The forest darkens in shame.
Bones scattered along the path.

Until dawn, the denizens wield blame,
Reluctantly, you search and invade,
Nothing remains in the hearth.

The Path Goes On

'Twas deepest winter
In an ash-grey forest, scattered with snow,
Each breath a splinter
Of sharp ice, striking the lungs blow by blow.
Amongst the dull leaves
Leeched lank, of their vitality and glow
Something old still heaves
And creeps, through shadows disarmingly slow.
'Tis a formless creature that all travellers on this path know.

Scales, we beg, please fall from our eyes of stone,
Despite this surrounding, the summer begins.
Why, we plead, does the sovereign sun spare us alone,
No matter how much we offer our own skins.
Here, we sigh. Are the remnants of our throne,
Sprinkled with simmering ash and broken javelins.
For a brief moment, the wind whips at our shins.

Panic flares, and thoughts return to what may scuttle and grow.
We turn with breath baited but all there is to see
Is the charred and twisted form of a crab apple tree
So we solemnly begin, sore-throated, to untangle our knotted woe.

For now, we've left the forest. At least, we hope that's true.
We do not spin this yarn as an attempt to pry pity from you.
Many know this tall, tall tale or one that means the same.
Some may gleam no meaning, but there is no need for shame.
We hope, with deathly gripped sincerity, that you never have to tell,
A story of that forest where many-headed monsters dwell.

Begin

Every journey must end.
A cliché begrudgingly accepted.
With this moment, I now send
A message, perhaps unexpected.

Beginning with the End
And ending on a new Beginning.
A fairly common trend
From smug poets grinning.

I scribbled notes and filled blank pages
With a plethora of perfect endings.
Forget the rhythmic rhyming stages
And prophetic pencil-crafted pretendings.

The chapter does not Begin because it cannot End.
Yet every day I begin anew to fight, to feel, to fend
Off those demons that can never truly bend.
So instead, I've decided, that I'll make this demon my friend.
I'll ridicule it night and day until its mind I'll rend,
And if anyone needs to do the same… I've got some poems to lend.

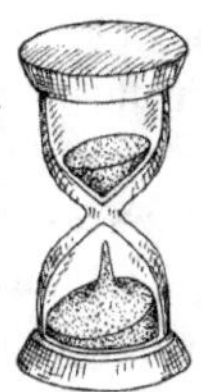

www.ingramcontent.com/pod-product-compliance
Lightning Source LLC
LaVergne TN
LVHW021314200726
843509LV00012B/1906